ghost
stories of
the south
west

Tony Wells & Melanie Warren

Published by Broadcast Books 4 Cotham Vale, Bristol BS6 6HR in association with BBC Radio Bristol.

Copyright 1994 Broadcast Books.

The BBC Radio Bristol series, GHOSTS, first broadcast in December 1994, is based on selected stories from this book. The views in this book are entirely those of the authors and are not necessarily those of BBC Radio Bristol.

Cover Picture:
A stone angel from Arnos Grove Cemetery, Bristol.

Photograph by Stephan Beese

Book and cover design by Edmund Crewe

Printed and bound by the Short Run Press, Exeter.

isbn 1 874092 25 7

Introduction

This book contains a mixture of ghost legends and real cases where real people have had experiences for which no natural explanation could be found. It will be obvious which type of story is which. The legends have been selected with care, for although there is no way of testing the truth of these stories, they fall into a consistent pattern with similar cases for which accurate modern reports exist.

Ghost phenomena are of course intimately linked to the question of whether the human consciousness survives death. Even in today's scientific and technological society there is a constant interest in this subject and in the wider aspects of the paranormal. Some might say that it is precisely because of our modern, high-speed world that we are interested in things of the mind, and in things of the spirit. Opinion poll surveys show that in Europe there is widespread general belief in the reality of many kinds of phenomena which most scientists dismiss out of hand.

And yet the foundations for paranormal research were laid down over one hundred years ago by eminent scientists and extremely hard-nosed sceptics. Two of the most notable scientists were Sir Oliver Lodge and Sir William Crookes – widely respected men who worked in both conventional science, and the unconventional area of paranormal phenomena. At that time the principal focus was an attempt to determine whether it could be proved that there was life after death. The claims of spiritualist mediums were rigorously tested. Some mediums seemed to produce a whole range of physical phenomena, ranging from the ability to levitate, to making musical instruments play by themselves. All mediums claimed to be able to communicate with the dead, and to bring back messages which had meaning to the living.

The last hundred years have witnessed the widening of the scope of areas to investigate. Scientists continue to theorise the possibility of 'classic' phenomena such as telepathy, clairvoyance and telekinesis (moving objects by force of will), and set up laboratory experiments to test them. Much of this work is classed as 'parapsychology', and cases of such classic phenomena usually fit into recognisable patterns of events.

The poltergeist phenomena described in this book are an example of this. A very famous case of poltergeist phenomena was the Enfield Case, which began in 1977. Apart from the 'usual' frightening display of objects being seen to move by themselves, pools of water appearing, and thumping and banging noises, there were more sinister developments. 'Janet', one of the daughters of the family in Enfield, would often speak in a voice unlike her own. She would also appear to go into a deep trance, and marks would spontaneously appear on her skin. Levitation was also reported. One of the principal investigators, Guy Lyon Playfair, wrote about the case in the book This House is Haunted. One of the peculiarities of the case was that when the family went on holiday, they fully expected to have the poltergeist 'follow' them. However, during the period away, their time, as in the *Possession?* story was completely incident-free. This is surprising because the conventional wisdom in poltergeist cases is that poltergeist activity follows the person, usually a teenager, who acts as a 'focus' for the disturbances.

However, the field is wider than these classic phenomena: UFOs, numerology, earth mysteries, out of body experiences – the list is continually growing. Although again the incidences can be divided into recognisable patterns, witness statements are often obstinately at odds with press stories or received thinking.

The story of the UFO's at Warminster has its echoes in the famous case of the phantom Blue Bell Hill hitchhikers, which occurred in Kent in 1965. Four girls travelling by car were driving down the hill, when they collided with another vehicle, and three of the four girls died. One of the girls was due to be married the next day. The press made much of this episode over the years, and every time something unusual happens on the hill it is generally attributed to the spirit of the dead girl. One can smile at this, but there have been a number of unusual incidents on the road. In the mid 197os a driver from Rochester was convinced that he had hit a young girl, about 10 years old, on the hill. He stopped, carried her to the verge, and rushed to fetch help. On returning he found she had disappeared.

There have been several similar incidents, and the curious thing about the witness statements is that they bear no resemblance to the press stories. The girls are usually described as being very young. There have also been reports of an old woman in the area, said to disappear suddenly before people's eyes. It is all this that makes Blue Bell Hill such a good example of statements differing from press reports that the incidents seem all the more convincing.

The nature of much of these phenomena makes it possible for the non-scientist to make his or her observations and thereby a real contribution to the subject. Ghost phenomena are of course in this category too.

Since the first investigations, the basic techniques for investigation have not changed. It is still vitally important to rule out natural phenomena and to guard against people playing tricks and pranks. There are now more and better instruments for observing happenings. One example is the widespread availability of video cameras both for domestic use and for surveillance. This is already beginning to show positive benefits. Many interesting images of apparently paranormal happenings have been captured on video tape – images which were not at all expected by the camera users.

At this point the sceptical reader will be asking the question – why is it that after such a long time of investigation, the the existence of ghosts and related phenomena is still unproven? The answer is the problem of repeatability. Two years ago a very exciting video of a large door in Dover Castle shaking itself violently for 30 seconds was taken. Since that time it has never been possible to recreate the circumstances that caused the door to shake. That is the goal of those investigating the paranormal – to try and find out what factors trigger circumstances such as the shaking of the door. It might then be possible to begin to unravel some of the problems which have baffled and frightened us since the dawn of our history.

Some of the stories are marked as real cases, but the names have been changed. When paranormal events occur in private homes, the occupants are usually less than enthusiastic, and rarely seek publicity. We have respected these wishes. Our code of conduct dictates that our work is strictly confidential and our results are not revealed to anyone not directly working on the case. Some people were happy to reveal the information about their case for this book, but not their names or other identifying features. For this reason, sometimes locations have also been changed.

This book has been produced with the help of ASSAP (the Association for the Scientific Study of Anomalous Phenomena). Many of the cases included have been collected by ASSAP investigators, who work in a voluntary capacity in collecting as much information as possible about the events which are reported to them.

If anyone is inspired by this book to let us know about any paranormal experiences, or wants to find out how to become an investigator, they should write to us at ASSAP. We will be pleased to read and answer your letters.

Tony Wells & Melanie Warren, ASSAP

Acknowledgments

The authors wish to thank Olwyn Barker, the Marquis of Bath, Lisa van Bemmel, Jane Cooke of the Old Vic Theatre Company, Bristol, Karin Cross, Benny Gibson, R.A. Gilbert, John Humphries, Claire Kiener, Maurice Lee, Joan Turtin and Sue of the Wackum Inn, Philip Steff, Jane Tapley of the Theatre Royal, Bath. Thanks are also due to fellow investigators Terry Cox, Joanne Darwood, and all executive members of ASSAP for their help in providing material for research, and to the many others who preferred to remain anonymous, for their kind assistance in the preparation of these stories.

We would also like to thank the ghosts, without whom...

Picture Credits

The Lamb Inn	by R.A.Gilbert
The Ancient Ram Inn Longleat Victorian Lady (photograph of sketch by Philip Steff)	by Tony Wells
Warminster UFO	by June Cameron
Brockley Coombe The Wackum Inn Theatre Royal Bristol	by Stephan Beese

More About Ghost Hunting

If you would like to find out more about the investigation of ghostly activities, or perhaps you would like to report phenomena you have come across, you can contact ASSAP (The Association for the Scientific Study of Anomalous Phenomena) at:

St. Aldhelm, 20 Paul St. Frome, Somerset BA11 1DX tel/fax: 0373 451777. Membership and enquiries to Hugh Pincott.

Experiences and sightings can be directly reported to the authors at the above address.

The objectives of ASSAP are to study, in a scientific manner, a wide range of anomalous phenomena, and to inform the public about these controversial subjects. The Association holds no official views and encourages its members to be open-minded about the subject.

The activities of ASSAP are concentrated on the investigation of apparently paranormal phenomena which members of the public report to it. Training is offered to investigators. and many ghost watches have been organised – some with dramatic results. ASSAP also researches extensively into other associated subjects, such as hypnotic regression.

There is an ASSAP newsletter issued four times yearly.

The Authors

Melanie Warren

Melanie Warren has spent several years exploring the paranormal, and has taken part in many 'ghost hunts', especially in Cumbrian castles. She is a regular contributor to ASSAP's publications, and has made several appearances on T.V. and local radio.

Tony Wells

Tony has been fascinated by the subject of ghosts and the paranormal for many years. When he is not working as a computer consultant he is a very active member of ASSAP, spending several evenings a month on ghost hunting projects with his colleagues. This includes working with mediums, telepathy experiments and making artificial ghosts. The purpose of this is to try to discover the underlying mechanisms behind apparently ghostly phenomena. He has also begun running the first evening classes in the UK on the paranormal. He makes regular appearances on radio and T.V., and has just published Ghostwatching (published by Virgin Books) with his colleague and UFO expert, John Spencer.

Contents

The Lamb Inn, Bristol

The Lamb Inn stood at the end of Lamb Street in Bristol, close to Lawfords Gate. It is one of the oldest areas of Bristol, and shows up on seventeenth century maps as having been at the furthermost eastern edge of the city. Only some old street names and a few eighteenth century buildings have survived redevelopment, and the Lamb Inn itself was demolished at the beginning of this century. Another equally gloomy looking inn was built on the site, and is still there today. It is the site of one of the most remarkable and best-documented hauntings ever recorded.

The account of the Lamb Inn poltergeists was written by Henry Durbin, a respected chemist living in Bristol in the eighteenth century. He described his eyewitness accounts of the events that begin in the winter of 1761, but he ordered that the manuscript should not be published until after his death as he had already been ridiculed by the press for investigating these events. His posthumous publishing of his account is interesting, and improves his credibility as a witness, for if his motive had been simply to seek publicity for his own ends, he would certainly have published in his lifetime, and probably very quickly after the event.

Henry Durbin's story begins on December 18th 1761 when he heard that Mr Giles, the proprietor of the Inn and two of his children were suffering from some extraordinary incidents. On his first visit he witnessed scratch marks appear on the arms of Molly, Mr Giles' daughter. She complained that it felt as if someone had run a thumbnail down her arm. It hurt as it happened, and smarted for a time after. As

Henry looked on, he saw her skin depressed by some unseen tool, and rise again, and a red weal appear. At the time this was happening, Molly was trying to sew, and Henry was convinced she was not cheating by using the needles to cause her scratch marks. Dobby, Molly's sister was also beginning to complain of similar problems. They also reported seeing the fingers and hands that were causing these peculiar marks.

Four days later, Henry reported that Molly again had trouble, this time with her knitting. Every time she tried to knit she complained that her needles were being interfered with. As Henry watched, the needles were tugged from her hands and pulled through the stitching. He tried to replicate this effect but found that Molly's stitching was so tight it was difficult to pull the needle through the wool. He also reported that more scratches appeared on Molly's arms.

Two days later, on Christmas Eve, the story began to take a new twist. In addition to the scratch marks, the tugs on Molly's knitting, and some annoying scratching and rapping sounds, objects in the house had begun to move of their own accord. The curtains raised and lowered themselves as if on pulleys, and the chamber pot whirled around the room several times. (It's to be hoped it was empty at the time.) Henry and a colleague again watched Molly's knitting needles operating by themselves, and tried to spot any trickery, but Henry seemed convinced that Molly was not faking the episode.

On January 5th, at eight in the morning, Henry and one of the staff, a nurse, were witnesses to an extraordinary incident. A wine glass rose a foot from a chest of drawers and flew across the room, striking the nurse's hip. It must have struck with force, for it left a bruise which was black and blue. Henry was so amazed he said to himself, 'Do I see what I see?' A short time later a similar incident happened with a cup in Molly's hand. As he had his eyes on the cup, it was snatched from her hand and thrown four feet into the air.

On Sunday the 10th of January, the phenomena underwent a new development. Molly and Dobby were pinched, Molly on the toe, and Dobby on the nose; this had happened before, but this time they both heard a voice say three times 'I'll follow you'. Things were generally becoming more violent; that day, Molly was found to have four pins pushed into her skin. The next day a pin was rammed so hard into her leg that it was bent with the force and it must have been extremely painful to remove it.

Saturday the 23rd of January (this account is verbatim from Henry's report), Mrs Elmes spoke to the invisible tormentor, when it was knocking and scratching, and said 'Art thou a witch? If so, give scratches;' which it did. This was the first time of asking any questions. It beat Molly's breast at the same time.

After asking more questions, it seemed that their tormentor was 'employed' by a specific person, although Henry's account gives no name, and they were given no reason for their persecution. The next day the nurse attempted more communication, and it was beginning to be clear that the answering voice was that of a woman. It sometimes refused to answer questions, and was not always heard by all in the room, but Henry's story makes it clear that there was a

The original Lamb Inn as it was before demolition in 1905

voice, coming from some unknown source, and it was definitely answering questions. A more effective form of communication was by means of non-verbal replies, or as Henry calls them, 'scratchings'. One message received was that the incidents would run for a total of forty weeks.

By mid-February the questioning was getting more sophisticated: some clergymen had asked questions in Greek and Latin and had been given sensible replies. This of course was a source of great wonder and excitement.

Throughout this time, Molly and Dobby were still plagued by bites and scratches: a week earlier Molly had suffered over forty cuts on her arm, face and neck. The tormenting by now was almost continuous. Molly was sent away to Kingsweston for six weeks, where she had some relief from the tormenting, but as soon as she returned on May 7th the violence on her began again. Her father decided that she must be sent away for the duration of the violence, which they expected to last until the end of 1762, as the voice had told them the haunting would last for forty weeks. Molly was sent to Swansea, and for a few days it seemed that the violence had diminished somewhat – Dobby was no longer being bitten and cut and not so many pins were being pushed into her skin.

The children weren't the only ones to be afflicted by the haunting: Mr Giles had also suffered several unexplained incidents with his horse-wagon, always at the same spot on the road to Bath. On the 12th of May, one of the horse-leathers broke and he had to stop to fix the problem. On returning to his carriage chair he saw a woman dressed in a cloak standing by the carriage. Convinced that she must be the person who had been tormenting his household, he was so disconcerted he did not have the courage to speak to her. He drove on, and looked back, but she had disappeared. This whole incident had occurred in daylight.

Then came disaster. Shortly after his meeting with the mysterious cloaked woman, Mr Giles complained of feeling feverish and ill, and four days later he was dead. The rapidity of his illness seemed to be a surprise to everyone. There is no suggestion in Henry's account that Mr Giles' death was attributed to the 'witch'... but he did state that the doctors thought his disease was rather uncommon.

For two months after Mr Giles' death all was quiet – no incidents were reported. However by June 7th Dobby was complaining of the return of violence – pins and skin marks again. Three weeks later Molly returned, the violence continued for her too, and one evening a few days later she was strangled by an unseen hand and remained senseless for half an hour.

The incidents continued beyond the predicted forty weeks, and on November 27th 1762, a year and a week after the troubles began, the voice told them that it had been re-hired to torment them again, but the troubles would not last long.

Desperate to stop the problems, Mrs Giles resolved to visit a white witch in Bedminster to ask for assistance. Without prompting, the woman told Mrs Giles, and two of her neighbours who accompanied her, that there had been horrible witchcraft in the house, a man had lost his life through it and a woman in Gloucestershire had been paid to cause the events to happen. At this place in his narrative Henry pointed out that most of this information was already known about, and it may not have been that difficult for the woman to have made these statements.

The woman was not sure whether she could help, for she said that the spirit of Malchi was involved, and he was extremely powerful. Incidentally, the unwanted occupant at the Inn had given the name Malchi to Henry many months before. The white witch needed an experiment to be performed before she could be certain of curing the problem. She asked them to take Molly's and Dobby's first urine of the morning and boil it over the fire. If when it boiled the colours of the rainbow appeared, then a cure was possible, and this could be done from the witch's home.

Back at the Inn they tried the experiment and reported that beautiful colours of the rainbow came from it.

Henry reported that from that moment no disturbances were ever reported again.

Epilogue

A copy of Henry Durbin's account can be found in the Bristol Central Public Library in the Reference section. The account was republished in 1971 under the title Witchcraft at the Lamb Inn by Vance Henry Publishing and with an introduction by R A Gilbert, and this is the copy held in the Library. It is one of the few records of a long-lasting case made by an eyewitness. Henry Durbin attempted to narrate the events as they happened, rather than colouring the story with his own beliefs. An interesting feature was that the occupants of the Inn tried to talk to the unwanted guest as if it were a human being, and had some kind of intelligence. What was even more interesting, it actually replied. These features add up to a remarkable milestone in the analysis and understanding of cases.

With more than two hundred years of hindsight we can look back at the Lamb Inn case with a slightly different perspective. We can see that it is possible that some of the incidents witnessed could have been attributed to trickery on the part of Mr Giles' children. But there were plenty of episodes where the children could not possibly have been involved. We can also see with hindsight that it is a classic case of a high-energy poltergeist haunting. When comparing the Lamb Inn with a more modern and well documented case such as the 1977 Enfield Poltergeist (see introduction), it was made clear that there were occasions where children were known to be playing tricks. But the point made in the Enfield case was that they could not possibly have staged all of the events, and this was also the case with the Lamb Inn.

There is one other aspect of the case that makes it similar to the Enfield episode, and that is that when the children were removed from the site of the disturbance, the number of reported incidents dropped, or they stopped completely. This does not fit well with the usual perception that some people are a focus of the mischievous energy, and that it follows them around. In both the Lamb Inn and the Enfield cases, when the children were removed from the location, the problems stopped for those children.

The question remains: how much of the Lamb Inn case was fancy or foolishness on the part of Henry Durbin, how much was the faking of events by the children, and how much by some unknown agency at work?

The Wrexham Drive Poltergeists

A house doesn't have to be old to be haunted. In recent years there has been a plethora of news stories about haunted council houses, seldom more than forty years old. It's easy to claim that the tenants are making it all up in a bid to be rehoused, but the following case shows that such scepticism is sometimes inappropriate.

How normal and inoffensive do the houses in your street appear? Perhaps you can't imagine anything strange ever happening behind those neat front gardens and tidy looking windows... Such a house belonged to the Ripley family in Wrexham Drive, near Bath. But in 1966, their peaceful lives began to be disturbed.

One day, the Ripleys' 22 year old son Paul was inexplicably pinned to the wall in his bedroom, as if someone were holding him there physically. He was unable to move for several more minutes, through fear. Then, just as suddenly, Paul Ripley was released.

Several days later, Mrs Ripley began to notice a man's shadow falling across the landing as she made the beds. Strange lights hovered around the beds and walls. Then Mrs Ripley and her 29 year old daughter, June, watched in amazement as a lampshade rocked itself backwards and forwards. Door handles were seen to move up and down, doors would bang shut for no reason, and even locked doors and windows would be found open.

The only person who didn't witness anything strange was Mr Ripley, but for the rest of the family the situation soon became terrifying and unbearable. No one was prepared to set foot in the rooms upstairs, and June was so frightened that she had to visit her doctor, who was only able to recommend her to a nerve specialist. Paul moved out altogether, refusing to return. It seemed as if the only answer was to exorcise the house, and the ceremony was performed by an Anglican priest who successfully exorcised the poltergeist ... for a time.

Nine years passed quietly, and then, in a similar council house just a short walk along Wrexham Drive from the Ripleys', a young couple began to be terrorised by a similar pattern of events. Helen and Tony were young newlyweds and the proud parents of a small baby son, Julian. They had been offered the council house in the summer of 1975, and were happy to move in. But within days of their arrival, they began to change their minds.

An unseen hand threw objects about the room. Doors banged suddenly, voices whispered in corners. One day, things came to a head. Baby Julian was lying in his cot when all of a sudden a cassette recorder launched itself into the air and was hurled across the room, hitting the wall just behind the baby's cot. Fortunately the cot was not closer to the wall, or the heavy machine might have crushed the child below.

That was enough for Helen. She left the house with the baby and moved back in with her mother, leaving her husband to cope on his own. Then the frightening episodes began to get more violent, with one door banging so hard that it was almost ripped off its hinges.

Tony became increasingly unnerved, and one day poured out the story to a colleague at work. Interested to see for himself what was happening at the house, his colleague agreed to stay overnight and give Tony some moral support. There was plenty to see. Within the first few hours of arriving Tony's friend saw the kitchen door start to rattle, quite of its own volition.

In the middle of the night, his workmate was roused from sleep in his bedroom by a lampshade propelling itself about the room and lights switching themselves on and off. That was the last time Tony's friend stayed overnight ...

Tony had to endure many months of this kind of thing before he was rehoused, and was able to get back to leading a normal life with Helen and their child.

The next set of tenants moved in, but didn't seem to report much in the way of problems. However, the poltergeist hadn't quite given up the ghost. In 1990 a single mother took up residence, with her 15 month-old daughter. Within weeks, the poltergeist was active again. Mrs Preston complained that her bed had been pushed into the middle of the room by unseen forces. She had also been bothered by someone pulling on the back of her jumper and on other occasions had heard tapping on an upstairs bedroom window. Soon the activity got more violent – furniture was thrown around and door locks were found smashed. Mrs Preston found, not surprisingly, that she needed to visit her GP and seek ways in which he could help her calm her nerves. She, too, has since been rehoused.

At the moment the Wrexham Drive poltergeist has quietened down, and everything is peaceful. But what can have caused these bizarre events? The hostility encountered by the Ripleys was thought to have been actions of a deceased 'evil relative', whilst the poltergeist that plagued Tony and Helen Preston is thought by locals to be the spirit of a miserable old man who once lived there. Local rumour describes him as a man who hated the human race in general, and children in particular, which would certainly explain the attacks on baby Julian. The theory is that he doesn't yet realise that he's dead, so one can understand his annoyance when he finds strangers – and their offspring – in his house.

But all of that is only speculation. From what we know about poltergeist activity, it seems to manifest itself when there is a high level of domestic stress, and certainly Helen and Tony were newlyweds with a lot of responsibility for their baby son. But none of the other people who were terrorised seem to fit the pattern quite so well. Another puzzling aspect to this case is the time span. Normally poltergeist activity seems to last only for a short time, rarely longer than a few months. However, there's always an exception to the rule... in this case, two houses on the same estate were affected, and the activity spanned several years.

Naturally, with two outbreaks so similar, and so physically close together, it's tempting to suggest that they are linked in some way: perhaps the entity which caused the original problem, and who was exorcised, simply moved house... is the Wrexham Drive poltergeist simply lying dormant, waiting to reappear sometime in the future, at some other house in Wrexham Drive? At present, the file must remain open.

The Ghost in the Computer

Poltergeists, it seems, are able to move with the times...

Anyone who has ever struggled with their computer may well have felt that it had an obstinate mind of its own. Many of us are used to unaccountable crashes wiping out hours of work, and grumpily put it down to our own clumsiness, or to electrical storms, or come up with a hundred and one other useful excuses... But how do we explain the following true incidents which happened recently on an industrial estate near Taunton?

In the spring of 1991, mysterious problems with the computers and electrical systems had initially exasperated, and then begun to unnerve the office staff. Phones began to ring continuously, but there was no one at the other end. Burglar alarms went off for no reason. The computers would flash their lights like mad fruit machines, before finally crashing into silence.

At first, it was thought that power surges were causing these manic bursts of activity, and the faults were reported to the Electricity Board. Engineers took the reports very seriously and installed sophisticated monitoring equipment on the electrical system. The surrounding roads were dug up, joints and junction boxes checked, phases and balances examined. It was long, expensive work, but none of it seemed to solve the problem - the disturbances continued.

Then the office phone seemed to develop a mind of its own. Several times it had connected itself to the Chairman's home phone, several miles away. It would ring away madly – but nobody had dialled him from the office. This, together with the bouts of continuous ringing, had the Telecom engineers completely baffled. Three times they replaced the entire phone system, carefully repositioning the equipment to avoid any electrical interference. But the anonymous ringing continued ...

Eventually, the computers were run from a generator, in an attempt to avoid any further power surges. For a week this was successful, until the day an ASSAP investigator came in response to the manager's desperate invitation. When Pauline arrived, all the computers promptly crashed once more. She had brought her camcorder to video an interview with an employee who claimed to have seen an apparition in the building. But the interview was a disaster: the camcorder seized up, the autocue wouldn't work and the batteries went flat after a few minutes. Undeterred, she returned to the office the next day with fresh batteries, only to find that during the night, a soldering iron had caused a minor office fire on the premises.

Despite the chaos around her, Pauline soldiered on with the interview, when all of a sudden there was an almighty crash. In a nearby room, a heavy photocopying machine had toppled over all by itself, frightening a member of staff out of her wits. The falling machine had bruised her arm as it had glanced past her, and had broken the work bench it fell upon. The woman hadn't even touched it.

On a subsequent visit, Pauline was accompanied by a friend who is sensitive to paranormal disturbances. While Pauline interviewed staff her friend remained in the car outside, but soon described a feeling of "tremendous psychic disturbance...". She saw shadowy figures passing through the external wall of the building in front of her – exactly where the office employee had described seeing his apparition. And she saw Pauline walk directly through a grey figure in the yard.

Her explanation was that there was great anger on the part of "elementals" or local spirits associated with the office site. who, she felt, objected to the two-year-old office being there in the first place. So she attempted to calm the spirits and told them it was best if they moved on, because the office was there to stay, whatever disturbances occurred. Strangely enough, that same morning, the atmosphere inside the building seemed to change for the better. Pauline's attempts at filming were incident-free, and no-one reported any strange electrical disturbances.

Had this last appeal to the spirits of the place worked? A few days later, Pauline rang the company secretary to check on progress, who in turn was delighted to report that there had been no further disturbances. The office was using mains power again, and telephones and computers were operating normally.

But we don't know if this is the full story. Decades of research show that poltergeist activity such as has been described always has a human focus. Under laboratory conditions it has been shown that such individuals – who are often under some personal emotional stress – can be made to move inanimate objects by will alone. It may be that poltergeist activity is the same human ability run wild, and it seldom lasts for very long. Did the quiet word with the spirits do the trick, or had the phenomenon run its natural, human course?

Karin Cross's Story

Karin Cross is a Registered Guide for the West Country Tourist Board, taking interested parties round the city of Bristol. She has lived in or around Bristol since she was born.

This story begins at a very turbulent time in her life. It was 1945 and Karin was expecting her first child. She was living in temporary accommodation while she and her mother looked for a suitable dwelling for herself and the baby. The flat was a ground floor flat in Cotham Road, Bristol, which belonged to an acquaintance of her mother's. Another friend of her mother's lived in the flat above.

The trouble began one day in August while Karin was cooking in the long, narrow kitchen. The wooden rolling pin was hanging by a loop of string from a nail in the wall. Suddenly, it flew past Karin's head and crashed into the door at the far end of the kitchen, as though propelled by an unseen hand. Unable to believe what she had just witnessed, she studied the nail from which the rolling pin hung – it was still firmly in the wall. The rolling pin, when retrieved from the other end of the kitchen, still had the loop of string unbroken at one end.

A few days later, Karin was resting in the bedroom, alone in the flat. She heard an almighty crash in the sitting room across the hall from her bedroom and she rushed in to investigate. A pair of heavy brass candlesticks which normally stood on a bureau were lying in the fireplace. The bureau was situated against a wall opposite the window in the centre of the room and the fireplace was at the far end of the room, several yards from the bureau. In an effort to rationalise the situation, Karin carefully studied her surroundings.

The outer front door, inner hall door bedroom and sitting room doors were all closed at the time. The sitting room sash window was down a couple of inches at the top, far too small a space for any creature to have gained access to the room. She checked the room to make absolutely sure no animal had got in, but there was nothing there. She realised that no animal would have the means or strength to move the heavy candlesticks so far anyway. The curtains did not reach as far as the bureau so they couldn't have knocked them off even in a gale, and in fact there was not even a breeze on that stuffy August day.

The next incident happened soon afterwards while her mother was staying with her friend in the flat above Karin's. Karin had gone up to see them and was standing talking to her mother while her mother's friend was in the kitchen making them some coffee. They were standing next to a bed-settee on which her mother had been sleeping. The light bulb in the overhead light above them slowly turned, detached itself from the hanging fitment and came down very, very slowly to rest on the bed-settee beside them. They both stood open-mouthed in amazement. This was the first incident where Karin had a witness to the goings on in the building.

The last occurrence in the flat before Karin moved away happened one day when her mother and brother had come for tea. Karin had laid the table and put out the food in the sitting room. Her mother and brother waited at the table while she went out to the kitchen to make the tea. There was a tremendous crash and she rushed back to the sitting room to see what had happened. She was told that a plate of sandwiches in the middle of the table had suddenly risen up in the air and been dashed to the floor, though neither her brother nor her mother was near the plate at the time.

Long afterwards, in 1972, Karin was staying with her brother and the conversation turned to various odd experiences the family had undergone. Her brother remembered the plate of sandwiches, saying how indignant he had been when fifteen years old to be accused by Karin of somehow knocking the plate off the table. His memory of the event was as vivid as the day it happened .

After long reflection, years later, Karin felt that she herself was probably the focus of the poltergeist activity. It was a period of intense difficulty and conflict in her life which was never outwardly resolved. Poltergeists are frequently associated with adolescents in a state of emotional tension, though similar kinds of activity may also involve persons in a higher age range who may be experiencing suppressed rage or frustration.

Possession?

Hands were grasping her throat.
Throttling. Strangling.
Something, some *thing* was holding her arms and her legs.
She could not move at all.
She could do nothing but scream.

But now she was awake.

It would be all right.

But no. Horrifyingly, she was still unable to move.
She could not even move her head.
She stared at the ceiling, the ceiling, the ceiling, the ceiling.
And screamed.

Now she was in the car.
In her night clothes
Going too fast.
Her father was driving too fast.
Her father was... terrified.

About twenty miles from Taunton stands a small housing estate built around four years ago. Howden Drive has two houses set in a cul-de-sac overlooking reclaimed marshland at the bottom of a little valley. The views are spectacular all year round. In 1992 two families moved into their new homes in Howden Drive, and, after a few summer barbecues, they began to get to know each other.

However, four months after they all moved in, an event occurred – a nightmare... perhaps. On the twenty-first of

October 1991 something happened which was to bring both families together – most unexpectedly and unfortunately.

It was five in the morning. Mary, the only daughter of the Steepleton family screamed. She woke both households. Mary yelled and shouted for over ten minutes continuously. No one could calm her. She did not seem to hear the entreaties of her parents. She could not explain what was the matter.

Her mother had to get a doctor. The telephone was out of action. She rushed next door to number 2 for help. Mrs Jackson, her neighbour, was already awake. She had heard the screams. Quickly, she showed Mrs Steepleton to the phone. The doctor lived over 30 miles away. It would be faster to take Mary to the nearby hospital. Help could be had there.

Mary was still shouting and screaming. By now she had worked herself into a frenzy. She was bundled into the car, screaming. Her father drove to the hospital as fast as he could. The little valley was shrouded in mist, hampering his progress. Once clear of the mists, he put his foot down.

Two minutes after leaving the house Mary stopped scream-ing. Five minutes later even her convulsive sobs subsided. She begged her father to slow down. By the time they got to hospital she was calm. Her parents wondered whether they should take her back home.

Mary said she was all right. It had just been a bad dream.

Mary's parents took her home, and back to bed. She slept very deeply and very long, missing school.

The doctor called in the afternoon to see how she was. He was the first to hear her story.

Mary said she had been asleep and had dreamt that hands had been grasping her throat, arms and legs so that she could not move at all. She could do nothing but scream. Then she had woken up but was still unable to move. She had stared at the ceiling. The next thing she remembered was waking up in the car, realising she was in her night clothes, and that her dad was driving at breakneck speed.

The doctor, unable to find anything physically wrong with Mary, pronounced her fit and well. She could go back to school the next day.

Life returned to normal.

Then on the twenty-third of November it happened again. At around five in the morning, Mary woke the household and her neighbours with another violent screaming fit. This time her parents decided to try and calm her down them-selves. But it was a long time – over thirty minutes - before Mary was calm. Again she had had the sensation of being strangled. Again she had woken up paralysed.

On the twenty-fourth of November it happened again. After this third attack, Mrs Steepleton went to her doctor for a referral to a counsellor. She was worried that there might be something wrong with her daughter's mind. Perhaps the pressure of starting at a new school was adding to the normal stress of a growing teenager.

Mary had two sessions with her counsellor. There was noth-ing wrong with her. The counsellor was baffled, and could only suggest hormonal imbalance as a possible cause of Mary's attacks.

There followed a terrible time for Mary.

Between October 1991 and July 1992 there were thirty-seven incidents. On thirty-seven mornings the hands grasped Mary's throat. On thirty-seven mornings something paralysed her. On thirty-seven mornings Mary screamed.

Mrs Steepleton began to note the screaming fits down in her diary. No obvious pattern emerged. The attacks occurred sometimes on Friday mornings. There were three attacks on a Saturday. Most attacks were in the middle of the week.

The attacks continued. The only respite was when the family went away for Christmas to stay with friends. Mary slept in peace. But three days after returning to Howden Drive, Mary had the same nightmare again. The pattern recurred when she went away on a school trip to France.

Two days after returning home, Mary suffered another attack... and another.

In July 1992 Mr Steepleton was asked if he would work abroad on a project that would take at least two years to complete. The request was made the night after Mary had suffered a particularly violent attack. The doctor had been called out to administer a tranquilliser.

Normally Mary's father would have turned down the offer. But such was their continuing torment that the whole family decided to rent the house out and move to America for two years.

The Steepleton family left England in August 1992.

Since that August Mary has had no further attacks. She is so happy living in America that she has pleaded with her father to stay another year. The family may take out American citizenship.

There seem to be no further problems at the house in the little valley. The people who rented the house from the Steepletons have recorded nothing untoward.

What could have happened to Mary?

There is no doubt that her experiences were real to her. The doctors were unable to explain the nightmares. There was nothing physically wrong. Considering her nocturnal experiences, Mary seemed extraordinarily well-balanced and mentally stable.

Her symptoms seem remarkably consistent – always the hands, always the waking paralysis. She always woke at the same time. The attacks only occurred at home.

There may be a simple explanation.

The estate where Mary lived was built on reclaimed marsh-land, in a valley sheltered from the wind. Mary may have been affected by excessive quantities of marsh gas in the atmosphere. It is known that air with a low oxygen content can cause hallucinations.

On the other hand, hallucinations tend to vary. Mary's experiences were always exactly the same. It is worth noting that no one else in Mary's family or in the adjoining family suffered in any way from marsh gas. There are resemblances between Mary's story and experiences reported by those suffering from or observing what is sometimes described as 'possession'.

The case remains open and is under current investigation – which is why the names have been changed.

Lisa's Story

Lisa was the manager of a privately owned residential care home on the outskirts of Bristol for a period of about six months. The care home is in a converted house that has belonged to the same family for about 200 years and is currently owned by two sisters, Pamela and Julie. Pamela and Julie were brought up in the house and Julie still lives in an annexe to the home. The annexe was built about fifty years ago and much of the interior of the original house has been changed about over the years. When Pamela and Julie agreed to let it out as a small residential home for people with various learning difficulties, the house was altered again to make it suitable, with heavy fire doors put in and extra bathrooms. The house is not in a residential area and is completely detached. It is surrounded by its own grounds, which means it is very secluded from outside noise or people.

Pamela and Julie had nothing to do with the management of the home, which, while Lisa worked there, was in her control. It very quickly became obvious to her that there was something very strange about the house. Lights were always going on in rooms where no-one had been and the doorbell would ring time and time again when there was nobody at the door. The clock in the dining room kept stopping, despite constant changing of batteries, and always at the same time. Lisa said it was always at 3.40 am and there didn't seem to be anything wrong with the clock, as it always went past 3.40 pm without incident.

During part of the time she was managing the home, there was only one resident. The resident, whose name was

Barbara, was a woman in her late thirties suffering from autism. While Barbara was the only resident, it was usual for only one member of staff to be present at any one time, which meant that Lisa didn't get to hear about incidents for quite a while after they happened. Gradually she became aware that she wasn't the only person who had strange experiences in the house.

One female staff member, who'd been working there for some time and was very reliable, told Lisa she didn't want to do the night shift ever again, and would leave if night shifts were obligatory. She had not only experienced lights going on and off, but also frequently felt that she was being watched. Once, when coming down the stairs quickly to see to Barbara, she'd glanced down and seen another foot on the stair next to her foot, though looking up, there was no-one there.

A male staff member said that on more than one occasion he had seen two men sitting in the conservatory, and on closer inspection, they had just disappeared. Lisa said that she also thought she had seen the men in the conservatory, but only their reflections in the glass.

The most frightening thing Lisa experienced happened one night when she was working on her own with Barbara, doing a sleep-in shift. Usually it was possible to walk through to the annexe where Julie lived, in the event of an emergency, but on this particular weekend, Julie had gone away. Lisa was entirely on her own with Barbara in the house.

Barbara has severe autism and doesn't speak. She does make some noises however, and is able to indicate distress, usually by inappropriate laughter, a sound hard to distinguish from her crying. You can tell she's distressed from her facial expression.

Lisa was planning to use the back room, which was the one furthest from the front door, as it was the room closest to Barbara's. She had put her night things up there ready and was sitting downstairs with Barbara in the room directly below. As we have already said, the house had been fitted with many fire doors, which also made effective noise reducers. Usually it was hard to hear anything in another part of the house.

Suddenly there was a very loud thud on the floor of the room above, which was the room Lisa was to sleep in. Thinking perhaps her alarm clock or some other object had fallen on the floor, Lisa left Barbara and went upstairs to check. Nothing had fallen on the floor, so she checked to see if the pipes ran under the floor in there, or if there was any other possible source for the thudding noise. She couldn't find any reason for it and so went downstairs again.

She hadn't been downstairs long when there was another loud thud. Again, she went upstairs to investigate and there was nothing there. This happened repeatedly throughout the evening until it was time to put Barbara to bed.

Barbara is unable to dress or undress herself, but usually acquiesces in the process of getting her to bed. On this particular evening she was very difficult, and seemed, in her own way, to be unhappy about being in her room. Once she is in bed Barbara usually has little rituals, like many autistic people, before settling. She sits up in bed for a while and makes various sounds before lying down to sleep.

Lisa went downstairs for a while and then heard loud noises coming from Barbara's room. She went upstairs again to check that Barbara was alright. When she got to Barbara's room, she immediately felt that something wasn't right. Barbara usually looks at you if you speak to her or come into the room, but she was positioned very oddly in the bed, with her fists clenched and looking very tense. She didn't look round when Lisa asked her if she was okay, but just stared away towards the wall. Lisa asked her again if she was alright, and she just laughed maniacally for about three minutes, apparently without drawing breath. Lisa had got to know Barbara's habits very well and she had never,ever heard her laugh like that before. Lisa tried to stay with her, but became so unnerved that she had to leave the room. She rushed downstairs and phoned up a close friend in an effort to calm down.

Some time later, Lisa went up to bed herself. She describes herself as an insomniac at the best of times and an incredibly light sleeper. On this occasion she had no expectation of sleep, but felt she should be closer to Barbara. She still felt that something was happening to Barbara, but that it was beyond her control, so she might as well try to keep vigil in her own room. She put all the lights on and listened to her personal stereo to try and block out the strange things that had gone on earlier.

The next thing she knew, it was late morning and she woke up having slept very heavily, not even waking to the sound of her alarm clock. Lisa said that for her, sleeping so heavily was the most unusual thing of all. Normally she wakes up if so much as a pin drops, and if she's even slightly on edge, she doesn't sleep at all. To sleep so deeply when she was so frightened seemed incredible. She felt almost as though she had been forced to sleep by something outside her control.

Thinking she should talk to someone about the strange events at work, Lisa contacted Pamela, the joint owner of the property, as Julie was still away. It was only then that Pamela felt it necessary to tell Lisa what had happened to the family when Pamela and Julie were growing up in the house.

From an early age, Pamela remembered there were always strange noises in the house. She was always hearing things on the stairs or in the upstairs rooms, in fact throughout the house and so did the rest of the family. The police were called on several occasions because the family heard noises in other parts of the house and thought it must be burglars. The police heard the noises too, and even called out the dogs to help them find the intruders, but there was never anybody to be found.

Pamela remembered that when she and Julie were teenagers, objects were often moved around while the whole family were out. On one particular day, they returned to the house to find large, man-size, sooty hand-prints across the ceiling in the kitchen, all down the wall, down the cupboards and on to the floor.

Night after night, Pamela would lie awake in bed waiting for the footsteps she dreaded hearing. Every night she

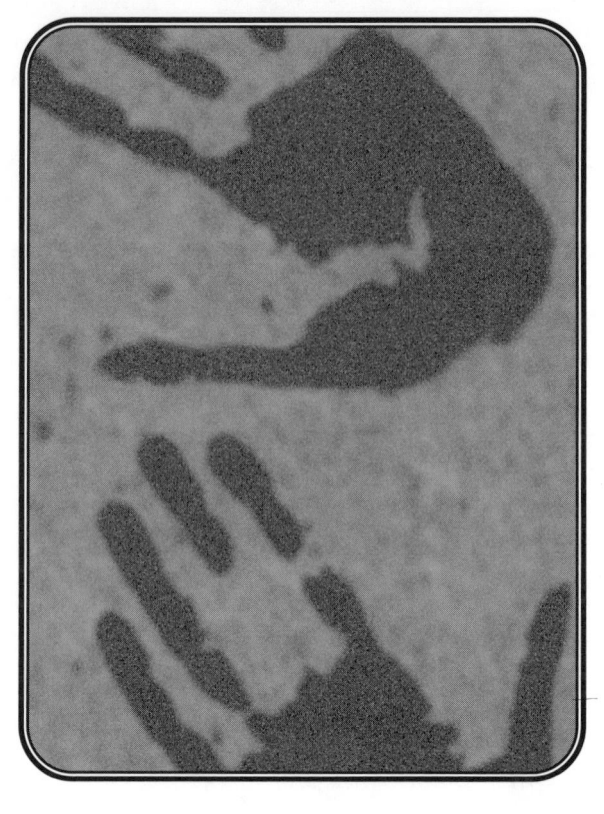

*An impression of the unexplained hand
prints that haunted Pamela as a teenager.*

would hear the front door open and close, followed by the inner door opening and closing, followed by the sound of footsteps coming up the stairs towards her room. Hiding under her bed-clothes, she would then hear her own door opening and someone come into the room, but when she steeled herself to take a peek, the door to her room was always shut and there was nobody there. Pamela's old bedroom was the room Barbara was now sleeping in.

Friends of Pamela and Julie's who came to stay would wake up in the night and insist on going home. Pamela remembered how her father got quite used to driving guests home in the middle of the night.

By the time she was fourteen or fifteen, Pamela decided to set up an ouija board to see if she could find the identity of the presence in the house. She told Lisa how frightening it was using the ouija board, as some force sent the pencil spinning towards letters without her touching anything. The spirit turned out to be a man, who let her know his name and that his death, which people had thought to have been caused by accident, was in fact a murder.

When Pamela and Julie grew up, Pamela left home for good, as she had no desire to live in the house. When she and Julie inherited the place, only Julie wanted to stay, and even she would only live in the annexe, a part of the house apparently unaffected. Julie is a devoutly Christian woman who refuses to acknowledge anything is wrong at the house, even though she lived through the same experiences as Pamela as a child, thirty years ago.

Lisa had to leave her job for personal reasons, but said that she had gone back recently to see Pamela and return her keys. Pamela told her that staff continued to complain regularly about unexplained phenomena in the building. Nobody will do nights on their own.

Farleigh Hungerford

Farleigh Hungerford Castle, eight miles from Bath, is just the kind of place you'd expect to find a ghost. The castle is in ruins, with just a couple of crumbling towers left standing. The only inhabitants today are the swirling white doves nesting in the battlements. A few buildings remain intact in the outer courtyard, the Chapel and Priest's House amongst them.

Like most aristocratic families with a long, traceable family line, the Hungerfords have a few skeletons in the closet. Agnes Hungerford, who inherited Farleigh from her husband, Sir Edward, in 1523, is the first Hungerford lady mentioned in the family records with an interesting history. Within eight months of inheriting the estate, she was arrested and later hanged at Tyburn for arranging the murder of her first husband, John Cotell. She had disposed of the body in the furnace at Farleigh Castle.

The next lady Hungerford – also called Agnes – had a terrible life. In 1536 her husband imprisoned her in the Southwest Tower with little or no sustenance. She smuggled out letters to Henry VIII's Chief Minster, Thomas Cromwell, begging for help. But all her entreaties were ignored. There was no-one she could turn to – even her chaplain had been bribed by Lord Hungerford to try and poison her. Were it not for the villagers taking pity on her and risking their lives to feed her secretly, she would certainly have perished miserably. As it was, she survived her wicked husband, who was executed in 1540 for treason and 'unnatural vice'. By a strange twist of fate, Thomas Cromwell was also executed for treason in the same year.

The tower where the second Lady Agnes was imprisoned.

It's not surprising that Agnes' ghost, according to legend, is supposed to haunt the castle. Maggie, who has worked in the ticket office there for a number of years, said she didn't know anyone who'd seen Agnes, but told us an interesting story concerning one of the tombs in the crypt.

As she was arranging some things on the counter one day, she was interrupted by a visitor saying: 'Excuse me, but she's very unhappy; you've got her on show and she doesn't like people staring at her'.

The visitor turned out to be an American Indian who described himself as being able to pick up on lost souls and other presences. Apparently one of the bodies in the crypt was unhappy about being on public view and she had requested to be covered over with green velvet.

Maggie didn't feel that English Heritage would particularly welcome the idea (or expense.) of covering one of the bodies in the crypt with green velvet on the whim of a passing tourist. The crypt under the chapel at Farleigh holds the lead inner coffins of six adults and two children of the Hungerford family dating from the sixteenth and seventeenth centuries. Four of the coffins have faces moulded onto them, probably taken from life masks, which helps to give the crypt an eerie atmosphere. Thinking that perhaps the creepy feel of the place had given the visitor hallucinations, she was startled when the man suddenly asked: 'Are you Maggie? If so, she gave me a message for you. You're not to worry about your night in the crypt, as she'll look after you.'

Maggie was utterly astounded. She had recently mentioned to her husband that she was thinking of spending a sponsored night in the crypt in an effort to raise money for charity. The event was not yet organised and there was absolutely no way that the tourist could possibly have known anything about it...

She found on questioning him that it was his first visit to England and he had only been in the country for a couple of days. He even showed her his passport so she could see for herself how long he had been in the country; as far as she could tell, the man was completely genuine.

Maggie says that in all the years she's worked at Farleigh, she's never encountered any ghosts and she is keen to suppress the idea of the spirit of Agnes Hungerford coming back from Tyburn to haunt any part of the castle. She thinks Agnes would bring an oppressive, evil atmosphere to the place and nobody feels that when they visit.

The only time visitors ever ask if Farleigh has a ghost is on Saturday mornings. Their sightings are always of a lady in the chapel next to the crypt, usually at about 11.00 am. Maggie always asks if they have noticed anything particular about the ghost; the one thing they all mention is her green dress.

Hunslet House and Church

Builders and electricians repairing old houses are often the first to report strange events – almost as if their activities are stirring an old building into angry life. This was the case at Hunslet House, a large, privately owned manor house approximately 30 miles from Bath. The current building on the site is over three hundred years old – yet the site is much older. It was even mentioned in the Domesday Book of 1086. But startled witnesses have reported strange sightings of a ghost much more recently than that.

Most often the ghost of Hunslet House is a friendly one, thought to be the deceased Lord William. He has appeared to dozens of workers on the estate, dressed in seventeenth century costume, and appears to be so solid and real that nobody was afraid – in fact many have claimed to have had perfectly normal conversations with him before he vanishes in front of their eyes.

The local legend is that Lord William refuses to leave the manor until a precious family plate which was hidden by an enemy is found and restored to its rightful place. Apart from appearing suddenly to people, he seems to be disturbed by building and restoration work, although his interference in these instances seems to be friendly, if mischievous.

A few years ago, two electricians were rewiring the house, a job that required a new cable to be run through a wall to the last room in the upper corridor. The first electrician fed one end of the cable through the wall, and shouted to his mate on the other side to start pulling. He sat back and watched as the cable began to move through the wall, but then looked puzzled as it speeded up, yard after yard whisking through the hole in the wall, until it had completely run off the reel and its end disappeared through the wall. He was annoyed with his mate for playing such a stupid trick and went into the end room to give him a piece of his mind - only to discover no-one there, and the cable was piled neatly on the floor. His mate, who had been gone for over twenty minutes to fetch a screwdriver, returned to find him scratching his head and wondering what could have happened. The ghost of Lord William had struck again.

Another group of workers reported a feeling of being watched when they were called in to restore the house chandeliers. It was a complicated job which involved removing the chandeliers for cleaning and restoration. During the removal, several pieces seemed to be lost, until they were discovered the next day on the floor of the ante-room, with an angry-looking Lord William looking over them. The plumbers also claimed ghostly interference with their work: when they replaced some ancient lead piping, the new pipe-work was found to have been wrenched out of place, and tools had mysteriously disappeared.

Lord William also has his helpful side. There is a story that an old lady visitor to the house felt suddenly faint in the grounds, and was unable to breath. All of a sudden she was helped to a bench by a young man in what seemed to be eccentric historical costume. He then disappeared in front of her – which didn't help her catch her breath much. The young man was later identified from portraits in the hallway as Lord William.

Close by the manor house is its church, parts of which date from the thirteenth century. It had been the private family chapel for Lord William's family, and many of the ancestors of Hunslet House are buried in tombs in and around the church. Life sized marble statues of the tombs' occupants stand around as if on guard... it has an eerie, some would say even evil atmosphere, with visitors reporting a feeling of being watched by several pairs of eyes. Some have seen a grey cowled figure lurking in the shadows... and one visitor had an even more violent experience. A young girl who had been blind from birth was brought on a visit to the church by her mother, but she refused to enter and became hysterical when her mother tried to coax her in. Perhaps she had sensed what people say they have felt and seen. All in all these hauntings are out of the ordinary, and perhaps apart from the friendly Lord William there are more sinister presences at Hunslet...

The Legends of Longleat

Longleat is one of the finest examples of late-renaissance architecture in England – and were we to believe all the stories, it would seem to have one of the finest collections of ghosts ever to be found in one place. Generations of the Thynne family have grown up in an atmosphere rich with ancestral legends and hauntings – but do these legends have any factual basis? Like most legends attached to stately homes and castles, the answer is that when sources are carefully checked, the truth is often very different.

One of the oddest legends about Longleat, written about in various books, is the grisly story that the house has carried a curse ever since it was built. It is said that Longleat stands on the ruins of a priory, and that the former residents, the monks, were not happy about the disturbance of their burial grounds, foretelling dire consequences... Several graves were indeed uncovered when Longleat's central staircase was installed, but we must doubt the curse's existence, for the family and Longleat has no more disasters than other families, and no doubt will continue to thrive for centuries to come.

Perhaps the most intriguing of the 'legends' written about Longleat concerns its most enduring ghost: the Green Lady. Ghost lore is full of White Ladies, or Grey Ladies – but the idea of a green lady piques the interest and certainly brings a strange image to mind. However, the explanation is quite simple – the Green Lady is thought to be the ghost of Lady Louisa Carteret, whose portrait shows her dressed in green. However, it would be interesting to know who first used this name for her, as neither Lord Bath nor any of Longleat's staff have ever heard her referred to by that name.

Wherever there's a ghost, there has to be a reason for its appearance, and the story of the Green Lady – or the Grey Lady, as she is known by the household, carries all the hallmarks of a romance. Back in the days of Queen Anne, the young and beautiful Lady Louisa was persuaded to marry the second Viscount, Thomas Thynne, a bad-tempered and heartless man. Very early in this miserable marriage, Louisa fell in love with a young man, and one night she smuggled him into Longleat. Unfortunately, the second Viscount discovered them together and challenged the young man to a

Longleat House

duel, which was fought along the top corridor of Longleat, ending in the young man's death and the concealing of his body under the cellar flagstones. Ever since then, the ghost of the Green Lady has walked the corridor, searching for her lost love.

A wonderful story, but legends have a way of transmuting over time, gathering more details with every telling, changing like Chinese Whispers. This legend, though, actually offered up some evidence. Earlier this century, when a central heating system was being installed in the house, workmen found a body under the flagstones in the cellar.

The present Lord Bath has lived at Longleat since 1953, but despite the abundance of ghost stories focusing on his home, he doesn't believe a word of them. His own bedroom is in the area where the Green Lady is reputed to walk, but he has never seen a sign of her.

As for the legend, Lord Bath has seen for himself how someone will claim to have seen a ghost, and how the claim will be embellished over the years, the story becoming firmer and firmer. In this case, he feels that several smaller legends have been combined to make the whole, and points out that several of the 'facts' are entirely wrong.

Lady Louisa Carteret was indeed young and beautiful, and her husband, the second Viscount, was certainly known for his quick temper. (He inherited at the age of four, which, as Lord Bath points out, is probably not terribly good for the personality.) However, Lord Bath thinks it's hardly likely that Louisa would have taken a lover so early in her marriage, and even less likely that someone in the Viscount's position would have deigned to fight a duel. This part of the legend may have come from a reference in an old book in Longleat's library, which mentions a duel having been fought at Longleat – but in Wigford Meadow, which is rather a different location to the top corridor of the house.

But there's no doubt that a body was found beneath the cellar flagstones – so who was he? And what really happened? Well, it's likely that Louisa, on marrying the Viscount, brought with her the customary 'faithful (male) retainer', who may have upset the other domestic staff by commanding all Louisa's attention and assuming an air of superiority. Naturally they would have complained to the Viscount that his new wife was spending far too much time with her confidant. And the Viscount, his temper roused by the onslaught of jealous complaints from his own faithful staff, may have incited them to get rid of the man as they saw fit.

Since childhood, Lord Bath has heard the story that someone died after falling down the main staircase – perhaps it was Louisa's faithful retainer? Perhaps he was pushed? It's probable that Louisa was simply told that her friend had suddenly left; given a woman's place in those days, she would not have been entitled to enquire further.

And so we see how a legend changes. With these new details, we have a whole new ghost story. The Lady Louisa might well constantly roam the top corridor, but there was no duel, and she does not search for her lost lover; she searches instead for her faithful retainer – perhaps because she doesn't believe a word of the tale she was told about

The main staircase of Longleat House

him going away. We also have a word of caution for the curious, intent on visiting Longleat to see if the Grey Lady really roams the corridors. We have been told that occasionally Lord Bath's secretary wears a long grey jumper in cold weather – in the dim lighting visitors have been heard to exclaim; 'Is that her ...?'

As for the body in the cellar – a skeleton was certainly discovered, dressed in clothing and boots from Queen Anne's day. It quickly crumbled, and the remains were placed in a hatbox and given a decent burial in the local churchyard, where, by a satisfying coincidence, the second Viscount is also buried. Perhaps in the future a new legend will appear – that on the anniversary of the young man's death, the two men appear, finally fighting the duel they were supposed to have fought in a ghostly attempt to settle their differences once and for all.

For those who may think that the Longleat files are a little too long on legend, and a little too short on real ghosts, there have been some interesting recent stories of unexpected apparitions seen by workmen in certain parts of the house...

Berry Pomeroy Castle

Berry Pomeroy has the reputation of being one of the most haunted castles in Britain. A spectacular ruin near Totnes, the castle has been totally uninhabited since about 1800. It is, however, very popular with visitors to the area and is a particular favourite with people investigating paranormal activities, having so many ghosts to hunt.

According to Deryck Seymour, in his excellent booklet "The Ghosts of Berry Pomeroy", there are fourteen different categories of paranormal phenomena which may be associated with the castle, all of which are well documented. These range from sightings of ghosts and hearing paranormal sounds, through to being touched by unseen hands and photographic failures.

Two former residents of the castle make the most interesting and apparently terrifying ghosts. Both are women, and both had tragic lives.

The White Lady is assumed to be the ghost of Lady Margaret Pomeroy, imprisoned by her insanely jealous twin sister, Lady Eleanor, because they were both in love with the same man. She was thrown into the deepest dungeon in St. Margaret's Tower and left to starve to death. She has been sighted in the dungeons, the tower and along the ramparts. She leaves those who see her completely terrified and with a feeling she intended to harm them in some way and according to folklore, to see the White Lady portends sudden and imminent death. This is obviously not so, as the few witnesses of recent years are still alive to tell the tale, but the legend is probably due to the feeling of dread she has invoked.

Sightings of the Blue Lady are recorded as far back as the end of the eighteenth century. To see her then was supposed to be a portent of the death of one of the castle residents. The castle has long been uninhabited, but the Blue Lady has been sighted a few times this century.

She was said to have been the beautiful daughter a of a former baron of Berry Pomeroy who was raped by her father and became pregnant. When the baby was born, she strangled it, and now haunts the castle as a soul in torment. There are tales of her trying to lure men to their deaths by appearing as a damsel in distress on particularly unsafe castle walls. Several men have nearly killed themselves in an effort to save her, while she beckons them on. She seems to have targeted men for these appearances, which isn't entirely surprising considering her family history.

The Blue Lady and the White Lady are ghosts of legend and sightings are very infrequent. However, Olwyn Barker and her husband, who run the castle tea-shop, tell us that visitors come to them all the time with stories of strange things happening to them in the castle. They have either seen the shadow of someone close by when there is nobody there, or become suddenly subject to irrational fear, their legs turning to jelly for no apparent reason. Some have felt "cold spots", which are unexplained patches of freezing air, felt even on balmy summer days. Sometimes cameras won't work properly, or else films become "misted" so that visitors' photos of the castle don't develop properly, even when other shots on the same reel are perfectly alright.

Mr Barker has seen one of the "shadows" himself, when he was alone in the castle after hours. On another occasion, one of the workmen who regularly carry out maintenance work at the castle was sitting in the cubicle in the Mens' Toilet. It was out of season and the castle was closed, yet he definitely saw the shadow of someone outside the cubicle. When he came out of the cubicle to investigate, there was nobody there. He now refuses to go in the Men's toilet, preferring to use the Women's toilet if necessary. Another workman had a conversation with a visitor outside the Men's toilet when he suddenly realised that the castle was closed and there shouldn't be anyone left in the grounds. When he looked again, the "visitor" had completely disappeared.

The approach to Berry Pomeroy Castle

Although many film "mists" and camera malfunctions may be assumed to be the fault of the camera owner, it would be expected that a T.V. company could get it right. However, Paramount Films had considerable problems when trying to make a programme about the castle to go out on T.V. on Halloween. They had persistent trouble with the film making, strangest of all being the lighting. The lamps worked perfectly well outside the castle, then ceased to function altogether inside the castle. They were carried in and out several times, each time working normally when checked outside, then not coming on at all inside.

Mrs Barker says that the tea shop itself is subject to unexplained phenomena. Visitors frequently report that someone has just grabbed their shoulder, yet turning round, there is no-one there. Mrs Barker herself has also had her shoulder grabbed - in the evening after the cafe had closed and all visitors gone home. This would be enough to terrify a less stalwart person, but Mrs Barker thinks we have more to worry about from the living than the dead. Most of the problems the curators have had in the past have been caused by night visitors to the castle. The castle used not to be so secure at night, and was used by various witches' covens and black magic practitioners, the evidence being left for the curators to clear. On one occasion, so much blood was found in the old kitchen area of the castle that the police were called in.

People are still sometimes given permission to conduct "ghost watches" at the castle at night, and sometimes strange things have happened, as with Paramount's T.V. programme. Most of the paranormal activity is confined to daylight hours however, so if you want to investigate, the opening times are from 9.00 - 5.00 every day from April Fool's Day to Hallowe'en. Meanwhile, Deryck Seymour has managed to collect enough stories to bring out volume 2 of the "Ghosts of Berry Pomeroy", as every week people phone or write to him to relate their paranormal experiences at the castle.

The Brockley Combe Ghosts

Most ghostly phenomena seem to occur in buildings, usually old buildings which have, as it were, seen much of life ... and death. But there are also many open spaces – groves, woods, even hills – in England and throughout the world which are associated with mysterious happenings and strange visitations. In many cases the stories of mysterious apparitions are firmly embedded as legend, but there are many modern sightings with a strikingly similar flavour.

Often the strong reaction of the witnesses makes it difficult to dismiss these country ghosts as pure illusion. So what are they? Are they the spirits of the dead returning to walk familiar territory, or some kind of time slip that only occurs under certain environmental conditions? Or are they, as some have suggested, a playback of some kind of recording which has been stored into the very fabric of the rocks and stones? Under certain conditions, and maybe with the right people present, these images are triggered, and so play back to the frightened witnesses. Or are they simply the product of an overactive imagination, heated by alcohol used to fortify the witness before venturing out into the stark cold of a windy night?

Just twenty miles from Bristol lies Brockley Combe. In the daytime, it is a well-used place, a leafy glen, beautiful, accessible, just the sort of spot that picnickers and hikers love to visit. However, at night it has a very different atmosphere. The lane which runs through the Combe is bordered by massive rocks and tall trees, and on a moonlit night the whole area is turned into a world of uncertain, shifting shadows. Even the most unimaginative can feel a shiver which is not entirely due to the chill of the night time air. At night, Brockley Combe is haunted.

Over the centuries the stories have been added to and embellished. Although in this modern world the tales may seem rather difficult to believe, they may, like many legends, contain a grain of truth.

A phantom coach, drawn by four black horses and driven by a headless horseman, is said to rush headlong at full gallop along the winding lane of the Combe. A certain Ben Brown, on hearing this tale, was not impressed. He had never seen and would never see a headless horseman – or any such tomfoolery. So, late one evening he set out along the lane through Brockley Combe with a spring in his step, fortified by a glass or two of strong ale. But, as time went on, and the church bell signalled midnight he began to think again, and decided to arm himself with stones. Those of us who have visited the Combe ourselves after dark may guess that the close proximity to the dismal woods was threatening. Ben was probably worrying about who or what might be lurking only a few feet from him in the trees.

Suddenly Ben heard the rumbling of coach wheels. By this time, he was thoroughly afraid, and hid behind a tree, clutching a stone. As the coach rushed past, he hurled the stone at the driver. But to his horror he discovered that it was not a headless horseman at all, but a driver who was very much alive, and carrying the local football team – who were not at all amused by his behaviour.

Brockley Coombe

Deciding that the team were not in a mood to listen to his excuses, Ben ran at speed down the lane, with the football team in hot pursuit, bent on revenge for the stone-throwing. Ben tried to outrun his angry pursuers. They were just beginning to catch up with him when, suddenly, there was another coach in front of them – a hearse-like coach pulled by four black horses – the phantom coach. Forgetting all thoughts of the chase, Ben ran in one direction, and the footballers in the other.

From that day, Ben was no longer a sceptic. We can safely assume that he did no more walking along Brockley Combe by night...

Ben, perhaps, need not have feared. The phantom coach and its headless driver seem to be indifferent to living spectators. A cyclist was once making his way up the lane, when he was startled by a coach bearing down on him at high speed. There was no time to move out of the way. The coach drove right at him ... and then passed straight through him. The only sensation he felt was an icy chill. Not surprisingly he fell off his bicycle, and it took some time before he was able to recover his wits, steady himself, and go on his way.

The coach and coachmen, however, are not the only mysterious apparitions to be seen at Brockley. The legends tell of a tall man in a long dark cloak. One evening in spring, a doctor was driving his horse-carriage through the glen, accompanied by a clergyman. By all accounts it was a fine night. As they drove along, the horse became restless and nervous, wanting to pull over to the side of the road. The doctor soon realised that the cause of his horse's restlessness was a tall man, clad in a black cloak, walking ahead of them. (The clergyman confirmed that he also saw the figure.) They drove on to a clearer patch, all the while following the tall dark man. The horse was continuing to give the doctor trouble: he had to use all of his skill to control the animal. As they reached the clearing, the figure disappeared. The doctor, more concerned with keeping the carriage going in a straight line, assumed that the cloaked man had moved off the road into the clearing. The clergyman, however, insisted that he had watched the figure fade away and vanish as if into thin air. He, at least, was sure that he had seen one of the ghosts of Brockley Combe.

The Famous Wackum Inn

The unusually named Wackum Inn, on Whitehall Road, Bristol, used to be called the Beaufort Arms, but was always known locally as the Beatum and Wackum. It was the first pub the miners would reach on the way home from the pit, and on pay-day it was a more popular stopping-off place than ever... By the time the miners emerged again, they had spent a large proportion of their wages, which is why their wives would wait outside to beatum and wackum....

A pub as old as this naturally has its share of ghostly legends. When the new proprietor, Maurice Lee took over in 1992, he knew about the pub's reputation for being haunted – he couldn't fail to know, for his regulars told him all about the stories. Of course, Maurice assumed that stories are all they were.

Moving in, with all the attendant bustle, went fairly smoothly... except for one inexplicable thing. When Maurice opened the old cellar door, his spaniel, who normally followed him everywhere, refused to follow him down into the cellar. The dog's fear of the cellar only increased with time. Many people saw how, at the mere sight of the open cellar door, the dog would shoot upstairs, tail between his legs. For a long time afterwards the dog would refuse to come back down.

Maurice was a practical sort of chap and thought no more about it. What couldn't be cured had to be endured... But about a year after moving in, the cellar made itself felt again. A building engineer came in to check out the foundations in the cellars, which consisted of a 'cold' cellar where the beer was kept, and a 'warm' cellar where there was a sink and other items of equipment. When he had finished his work, he took Maurice aside. Maurice was feeling a bit worried, for he thought that from the engineer's behaviour there was going to be some expensive repair work in the cellar. However he was taken completely by surprise when the engineer quietly explained that he was a bit 'sensitive' to atmosphere and that he thought the pub was being haunted by an old soldier. Whilst he had been working in the 'warm' cellar, he said, he had felt as though he was being constantly watched. He didn't know how he knew, but two names and a date had come into his head: George Blanchard and Herbert James, and '42', which was taken to mean 1942. The engineer added that he felt that Herbert James was the name of the old soldier, but he didn't know who George Blanchard was. Maurice didn't know what to make of this, and was so relieved that there were to be no expensive repairs that he dismissed the whole episode from his mind. But six months later, in September 1993, something happened that he was never to forget.

The pub had closed for the night, and Maurice was alone in the bar, busy cleaning up the night's debris in readiness for the following day. The routine was by now a well-worn habit, and as usual, just after midnight, he went down into the cellars to check the beer barrels and gas and wash away the waste beer.

As he was standing at the sink he had a distinct feeling that someone had entered the room. Assuming it was a member of staff, and concerned that they were standing there without speaking, Maurice tried to turn round to say something. But he couldn't – he found that he was rooted to the spot with fear. The atmosphere had turned icy cold and the hairs on the back of his neck had risen in response. Summoning all his courage he managed to turn his head a little. Standing there a few feet in front of him was someone he had never seen before, dressed in very odd clothes. He was dark, thin, and very neat, wearing a black moustache.

His waistcoat was especially unusual: it seemed to be an old-fashioned naval waistcoat, navy blue, decorated with white stitching and quarter-inch braiding, and it had a stiff upright collar. It also had no buttons.

Maurice was sick with fear. He turned around completely to face the stranger, but he had vanished. Maurice made a very hasty retreat from the cellar, and it was several minutes before he felt warm again. He admits to having felt petrified by what had happened, which seemed to have lasted much longer than the few seconds that had passed.

Could his visitor have been the the old soldier, mentioned by the engineer six months previously? Maurice talked over his experience with Jack, one of his regulars, whose daughter Elaine agreed to research the style of dress the soldier was wearing, once Maurice had made a sketch of it.

Elaine's research came up with an interesting discovery. Maurice's sketch was a near-perfect description of the naval uniform worn by the Yeoman Hussars – a naval regiment formed in Somerset in 1840. The docks at Bristol played a vital role during the Napoleonic wars and it became a renowned naval port, so it's quite possible that the Hussars

Maurice Lee at work in the haunted cellar of the Wackum Inn

were stationed there for some time. As for the date, '42'; it must have been 1842, rather than 1942.

If Herbert James really was a soldier of this naval regiment, just as the engineer had said, who then was George Blanchard? Another local resident was able to shed some light on that mystery. She is an elderly lady now, but remembers George Blanchard from her childhood – he lived a few doors from her, and was an old man when she knew him, but what his connection to Herbert James was, she didn't know. If George Blanchard was alive at all in 1842, he can only have been a very young child.

The old lady did remember visiting the inn herself many years previously. She was amazed to see a trail of wet foot-prints, of bare feet, leading from the sink in the cellar up the stairs before ending abruptly. These were visible for about an hour before drying out. Nobody else was around at the time. Is the cellar haunted by two ghosts independent of each other? Did Herbert James drown at sea during a naval battle?

We may never know the answers to these questions, because since that time, Maurice has had no further experiences in the cellar, or in other places in the pub, although other visitors have sometimes claimed that they sensed a certain atmosphere in the place. But Maurice openly admits that although he used to be sceptical about the subject of ghosts, he is not quite as sceptical as before...

The Haunted Thorn Hotel

Miles from any other habitation, the Thorn Hotel sits in a fold between the wild, bleak uplands of Exmoor. It is close by an old drover's road that bridges over the little river winding along the valley bottom. This was once a busy crossroads - some say the site of a gibbet, where luckless vagabonds and thieves would end up swinging in the winds that come beating up the valley.

The old house once belonged to a preacher and his two unmarried daughters, who in the way of dutiful Victorian spinsters had looked after him until he died. They lived out their own lonely lives in the house until their own deaths, within months of each other, in the 1940s. Since then the house had stood empty, its roof and floors falling in, and thistles taking over the garden. There were no buyers, until Mr and Mrs Cameron visited the area and decided it would make a perfect, get-away-from-it-all hotel. They made enquiries about the house in the village, and received evasive or disconcerting replies.

"Thorn House? There's nothing there that will hurt you..." One response was more direct: "Thorn House? It's haunted."

Mrs Cameron is an energetic woman and had decided, whatever the locals thought, to renovate the Victorian house and turn it into her hotel. Her husband was equally dismissive of the rumours. Soon a team of builders was appointed, and the house began to reverberate to the sounds of hammering and sawing - and that is when the troubles began.

Builders came and builders went. None could be persuaded to spend more than a few nights at Thorn House. They complained of doors locking and unlocking themselves, lights switching on when they had left them off, tools vanishing and reappearing, and of hammering and thumping sounds in distant rooms where there was nobody. Mrs Cameron once came back to find a terrified workman sitting in the garden, wrapped only in a towel. He had been alone in the house, and had taken a bath at the end of the day. The bathroom door had stood open, as there was no-one around – or so he thought. Suddenly he stopped splashing and soaping, and strained his ears. Two female voices were whispering just around the corner of the open door. He was unable to make out what they were saying – but they were definitely there. He leapt from the bath to the doorway - but the corridor was empty. The builder made his excuses to Mrs Cameron, and left the job.

She was getting a bit exasperated by this point - after all, she had never heard anything, and she loved the house. She then appointed two young electricians, friends of her son, to come up from London to finish the wiring of the attic rooms, and carefully avoided any reference at all to stories that might alarm them unnecessarily.

The boys, Paul and Alan, were just finishing the wiring, very late one night. It was pitch black outside, no moonlight, a November night of freezing rain. The work had gone well, but they felt uneasy in the lonely house and were glad to be packing up. Alan went downstairs to put a bag of tools in the boot of their car in the driveway. Then Paul saw that he had forgotten his pliers and went to catch him up, only to stop, terrified, in his tracks. Following Alan down the stairs, and vaguely visible in the black, was a grey shape. It moved out of the door after him. Paul tried to shout but his throat seemed to have tightened and shrunk, and the only sound that emerged was a squeak of panic. He rushed back to the attic window and saw Alan open the car boot in the drive below, with the shape looming menacingly over him. He found his voice at last, thrust open the window and screamed: "Alan – get into the car!" He then hurled himself as fast as he could downstairs, out of the door and into the passenger seat next to Alan. The last thing they saw before the car screeched out of the driveway was a second grey face at the attic window, which seemed to will them to go.

The next morning Mrs Cameron arrived from London to find the back door and attic window of the house banging open in the wind as the boys had left it. There were tyre skid marks in the drive, and a pair of pliers on the attic stairs. Understandably annoyed she rang the electricians up, but nothing would induce them to go back to Exmoor, not even to be paid.

Mrs Cameron soldiered on with the repairs herself, and eventually the house was finished and brightly painted. She invited an old friend, a priest, to bless the house – although what peace of mind that would bring to people who knew the house, she couldn't say. But certainly since the building repairs have stopped, so have the disturbances. Today guests come and go, refreshed after their peaceful stay in a lovely old house in the middle of the moors. Were the old ladies the cause of the trouble, resentful that their peace and their home was being disturbed? Nobody has heard or seen them since, apart from a child guest once, who innocently mentioned at breakfast that two old ladies had reached down to her in dreams...

The Swimming-pool Ghost

Stately homes and castles are not the only places to have their ghosts, and hauntings can occur in the most unlikely spots. Perhaps there are none stranger than the old Victorian public swimming baths in a major town in the South West, which has its own most unexpected visitors...

Over the last ten years there have been repeated strange incidents of poltergeist-like activity at the swimming pool. Footsteps echo up and down the empty corridors when no-one is there, lockers are opened and turned inside out, electrical equipment misbehaves, and, more strangely still, attendants sometimes hear the sound of shattering glass - and on going to inspect the damage, find nothing at all. These incidents seem to be centred around the Turkish Baths area, on the ground floor. The belief amongst the staff is that the disturbances are caused by the ghost of Bert, a masseur who used to work in the Turkish Baths, who one day suffered a fatal heart attack whilst at work.

In the late 1980s, John Weller became deputy manager at the pool. He was immediately regaled with stories of Bert the ghost, but he would only smile good-humouredly when he heard them. He was not the sort of person to believe such tales, sure that his leg was being pulled in the endlessly amusing game to his colleagues of 'ribbing the new boy' – especially as it was his job to walk through the empty, echoing baths last thing at night in order to lock up. After a year of lots of rumours but no ghost, John was more sure than ever that 'Bert' was simply a piece of folklore – until one evening, when some strange things began to happen.

It was part of his duties for John to attend public meetings to discuss the old building's future. Victorian baths up and down the country have been closed one after the other, as the public tires of pale green tiled swimming pools with the depths marked in feet along the sides, and begin to demand palms and wave machines. At the end of the long meeting, when everyone had left for the evening, it was left to John and Robert, a colleague, to turn off the lights and lock up.

This they conscientiously did, but as they were leaving the building John saw that one of the lights was still on. Surprised, because he was sure he had done the rounds most carefully – and cross at himself, he laboriously went through the unlocking procedure of the main doors again, turning off the burglar alarm, and went back inside the building .As he reached the Turkish Baths area, he suddenly heard a voice, coming from behind the door, asking him very politely; 'What are you doing here?'

John nearly leapt out of his skin. Was this Bert the Ghost? But then he realised that this was not a man's voice, it was a woman's ... His heart thudded in his ears as he waited for the voice to speak again. But there was no other sound.

After a few moments John remembered to turn off the light, and in the darkness he tried to convince himself that he had heard nothing at all, and it was simply an over-active imagination. It was late after all.

On his way back to the exit, he again walked past the same area where he had heard the voice. Feeling a bit of a fool for frightening himself and being so silly, he walked confidently past the Turkish baths and suddenly stopped dead in his tracks. 'What are you doing here?' demanded the voice again. This time John rushed out the main entrance where he heaved a sigh of relief, and hastily made his way to the nearest pub.

All was quiet for a few weeks. But one evening, John again had trouble with the lights when trying to lock up – this time in the main foyer. Again he had to go through the rigmarole of unlocking the main entrance and turning off the alarm before he could walk up to the switch and turn it off. He locked up once again and just as he was making his way down the drive, he turned around to give the place a last look, and to his astonishment, the foyer lights were on again. For a third time he had to go back inside to switch them off. This time they stayed off.

A few months later, John was sitting in his office working on a staff roster when he suddenly noticed that a memo pinned to his notice board was swaying backwards and forwards. He watched it with fascination and then saw it stop. John was rather perturbed by this, as there had been no draught, and no other obvious reason why the paper should behave in this way. He tried to recreate the same type of movement by blowing on the paper, opening and closing the office door, and finally rocking the notice board, but it refused to move in the way he had seen it move.

John was not the only person to have heard a woman's voice in the pool. Another employee once reported seeing a woman right in front of her in the Turkish Baths area. She was a slim, petite woman, wearing a long dark nurse's uniform and a fluted hat.

It turned out that the building was originally a public hospital, which had been opened in 1889. A few years later a swimming pool and Turkish baths were added. During these early days the hospital was run by Red Cross nurses, whose uniform in those days consisted of dark ankle- length dresses and a fluted hat which hung loosely down the back – exactly as worn by the woman seen in the Turkish bath area. In later years the uniform changed: the dresses became shorter and the hats more starched and upright. This makes it possible to date the sighting of this woman to having lived within about twenty years of the opening of the building.

During the Second World War, the place was used as a military hospital and 100 extra beds were added. The swimming pool was actually drained and filled with beds to act as a ward. During this time 400-500 soldiers and airmen passed through the doors, many of them flown from the Normandy beaches directly to the hospital, which served mainly as a casualty clearing station. During this time it was thought that the Turkish baths were used as a temporary morgue.

There are no easy explanations that fit the reported occurrences, despite the rumours which circulated before. The woman's presence seemed quite a peaceful one. Is she behind it all, including the paper moving on the wall in John's office? Or perhaps the rumours of changes to the old building disturbed Bert the masseur, who loved his work there so much that every now and then he shows his disapproval?

The Victorian Lady

Living in Bath is a spiritualist medium, Philip Steff – a man who devotes a lot of time to helping people who suffer from uncomfortable feelings and unexplained phenomena. One day he was visited by Peggy, who asked his help in solving a curious problem that had plagued her family for years.

When she moved into her house in Bath some twelve years ago, she had the very strange sense of being watched in her bedroom – from one particular corner. Although it alarmed her and made her nervous, Peggy never mentioned this feeling to a soul, not even to her husband, for fear of being laughed at. This situation persisted for many years, until at last matters came to a head. Peggy's husband, Bob went into hospital for a few days, leaving Peggy alone in the house.

She felt far too frightened to sleep in the bedroom by herself, and so made her bed downstairs instead. When Bob came home and commented in surprise on the bed in the living room, Peggy confessed her fears to him at last. But Bob didn't laugh. He had felt exactly the same, he told her. It soon turned out that not only Bob and Peggy but their son, daughter and daughter-in-law had all had that same feeling of being watched in the bedroom, and all had kept the feeling secret from each other. The joke was on them all.

Now that it was possible for the whole family to openly discuss ways to deal with the problem, Bob suddenly remembered reading and keeping an article about Philip Steff, which described a case in Bristol when he had helped someone whose room had a persistent, nasty smell. It was impossible to describe this smell, which would come and go mysteriously.

Philip was interested in Bob and Peggy's story and agreed to help. He came over with two helpers, and they immediately sensed that there were good grounds for concern. They asked Peggy's permission to perform a "sitting" in the bedroom, where they would try and contact the spirit which seemed to be generating the bad feelings. Philip invited Peggy's family to join in – but it was all getting a bit much for them. They decided to wait downstairs in the sitting room to await the outcome.

Minutes passed silently. Then after about half an hour Philip came down with his colleagues, and told them that the problem was solved.

The minute he had crossed the threshold, he had been met by the person inhabiting the bedroom. It was a Victorian lady who had lived and died in the same house over a hundred years previously. Her sad face appeared to him so vividly that he was able to sketch her later. She had been ill for most of her life, and had never really had much experience of the world before she died – so she had taken up residence in Bob and Peggy's bedroom in order to see a little more of the life she had missed so much, at second hand. However, Philip was able to persuade her that she really should be off to her proper place – wherever that may be – and she promised to leave.

Philip thought it would take about three days for the atmosphere to clear itself of her 'presence', but in effect it hap-

Philip's sketch of the Victorian Lady

pened much more quickly. That very evening the oppressive feeling of being watched had gone for good. The room felt completely different. It was, said Peggy, as if a light had been switched on in the dark, and when her daughter-in-law came round a few days later she, too, remarked on how different the room felt – and she hadn't even known that Philip had called and done his work.

Another strange aspect of this case is that an unpleasant looking white cat – nicknamed Emily – which used to unnerve the family by staring in at the kitchen window for hours at a time, vanished the moment Philip entered the house. They never saw it again. As both cat and Victorian lady vanished at the same time, Peggy named the lady Emily too.

The family were very grateful to Philip and kept in touch with him. He was able to perform a last service for the family a few years later, when Bob was dying in great pain in hospital. Through taking morphine to hold the pain back, Bob was suffering from hallucinations, and he was certain that there were three presences in the room with him. They terrified him, and he started calling for Philip.

Philip came over immediately and sat with Peggy and Bob, holding Bob's hand. He didn't do anything in particular, it just seemed enough for him to be near. Bob eventually calmed down, and Philip left the hospital, never to see him again. A few days later, at around three o'clock in the afternoon, Philip felt that Bob had finally died. When he got in touch with Peggy she confirmed that he had, in fact, pinpointed the exact moment of her husband's peaceful death.

There is no doubt that Peggy and her husband had been helped by Philip. But had the entire problem been caused by the Victorian lady that Philip drew, or was there something else which Philip was able to help eradicate? These are questions which have baffled investigators and many scientists since the 1860s when the belief in the ability to contact the dead became so widespread. Maybe one day, with more investigation – and if we learn to ask the right questions – we will get nearer the truth.

Theatre Ghosts

When you walk into the quiet of an empty theatre, and take a moment to look around and listen, the air seems to vibrate with the echoes of plays long gone. The theatre boxes are black beyond their velvet curtains, no longer crammed with applauding audiences. It's easy to believe that there are ghosts in every corner, and indeed, most theatres throughout the country claim to have at least one ghost, and regard them as part of the scenery...

The Theatre Royal in Bath, has been reputedly haunted for many years. Built in 1805, it is one of the most beautiful theatres in Britain, especially since it was lovingly restored some years ago. The fact that it looks much the same as it did when it was first built only adds to the generally 'haunted' atmosphere – but there's no doubt that some people have reported truly ghostly experiences in the building.

The most commonly seen ghost is the 'Grey Lady', so called because she appears in a long grey dress, with grey feathers in her hair, and smelling very strongly of jasmine perfume. Her costume seems to be from the eighteenth century, and the present staff believe her to be an actress from that time, They don't know her name – but they all know the legend behind her haunting of the theatre.

Over two hundred years ago, the Grey Lady was a popular actress, who often performed at the Theatre Royal. Although married, she had a liaison with a very regular theatre-goer who always sat in the same box, which in the eighteenth century would have been directly over one side of the stage. These boxes were most popular with special admirers of actresses, as they were perfectly positioned for throwing down trinkets and billets -doux, and generally carrying on amorous conversations between the speeches of the play. In the tragic way of such legends, her husband discovered the relationship, and did what the decent man did in the eighteenth century; he challenged his rival to a duel. Learning that her lover had been killed, the Grey Lady was so distraught that she hanged herself in a local hotel, the Garrick's Head. However, seemingly unable to relinquish the scene of her many triumphs, the ghost of the grey lady lingers on.

The Theatre Royal, Bath

Mysterious events have also occurred in the theatre itself, but whether they are associated with the grey lady is not clear. In 1948 the Christmas pantomime included a butterfly ballet, with the dancers dressed as tortoiseshell butterflies dancing around a large, illuminated butterfly in the centre of the stage. During the performance a real tortoiseshell butterfly appeared – curious enough in winter – and fluttered around the theatre. Every year since then, with only one exception – a butterfly appears at the Christmas pantomime.

There have been other strange occurrences: in 1963 a stage clock struck three o'clock – at precisely three o'clock – despite the mechanism of the clock having been removed first. At a subsequent performance the lights all dimmed at three o'clock again, although no-one had touched them.

Then two years ago, the Grey Lady made a most spectacular appearance during a performance of a play called, appropriately enough, 'A Moment Of Weakness'. And as if to disprove the commonly held notion that ghosts only come out at night, her appearance was during the Saturday Matinee.

The play starred Liza Goddard and Christopher Timothy, who were somewhat surprised, during their performance, to see a lady in eighteenth century garb sitting in a box which they knew full well was not occupied by the public that afternoon. In addition they also felt extremely cold, and although they gamely continued with the play, they were both quite shaken by their experience and told the staff all about it afterwards. Their description of the lady matched that of the many people who had been surprised by her before, and the staff took Liza and Christopher's story quite seriously, particularly as the box where they had seen the Grey Lady was the very one where her lover had been known to sit, night after night...

The oldest working theatre in Britain is the eighteenth century Theatre Royal in Bristol – popularly known as the Old Vic, after the resident theatre company. The company from Bath also often performed there. Theatre-going in the eighteenth century was a rumbustious and not entirely respectable pastime. The Old Vic in Bristol was forced to disguise its entertainments superficially as "A concert of Music" with comedies and farces interspersed between the orchestra performances, until 1778, when George III granted the theatre a royal license and thereby a surface respectability. The theatre was the perfect place to catch up on gossip and assignations. Servants would be sent ahead to "bag" the best seats for their masters, often an hour and a half before the performance – and the parties among revelling groups in the audience began well before the start of the performance at half past six.

Feasting and often rioting were part of the fun. Recent excavations of the floorboards beneath the old auditorium revealed, beneath the foot of dust, orange peel, nutshells and hundreds of discarded corks. There were ferocious iron spiked railings along the stage to repel assaults on the actors from enraged members of the audience, if the play was proving unpopular. But if the audience approved of a particular speech or actress, she would be required to repeat her scene over and over again. The whole stage and auditorium would have been lit by flickering candles, and

The front of the Theatre Royal (Old Vic) in Bristol

it is not surprising that as a result of such lively audience participation, most wooden theatres have long since gone up in flames.

The Theatre Royal is one of the very few eighteenth century wooden interiors to have survived. Jane Cooke is the senior scenic artist at the theatre, and has made many detailed researches into the theatre's history. She discovered that although Sarah Siddons did appear at the Old Vic, she was at the time based at the Theatre Royal in Bath, only travelling to the Old Vic three days a week. She spent four years at the Theatre Royal in Bath, and so could be responsible for the sightings of the eighteenth-century actress dressed in grey.

Sarah Siddons certainly didn't seem to have any great reason to haunt the Old Vic in Bristol; the popular legend is that Sarah's daughter died of tuberculosis when Sarah was working at the Old Vic, but it has since transpired that her daughter's death did not coincide with this period.

However, there is a ghost at the Bristol Old Vic, and there is another Sarah who Jane thinks is a much more likely candidate: Sarah McReady, a famous Victorian actress whose husband managed the Old Vic for several years. On his death, Sarah took over the job of Manager - not a job that was wholly acceptable for a lady of that time, but then Sarah was no ordinary woman. She was described in her old age as 'a Sybilline and eccentric old lady', and all accounts of her managing the theatre are of tremendous courage and fortitude. The Old Vic was her life for over thirty years, right up until her death in 1853. If anyone has a right or a reason to haunt the Old Vic, surely it's Sarah McReady.

Certainly the sightings of her sound more like a Victorian woman than one from the eighteenth century; the figure is in a corseted dress, with a high neck, and always black; Sarah McReady was a widow for over twenty years. Her hair is parted severely in the middle, which is a mid-Victorian hairstyle. Several people have seen her; so many that Jane has taken to keeping notes of her appearances, and these notes show that she only appears in areas of the theatre which were there in her time; never in the recent additions. She also seems to appear more often at certain times of year, which coincide with those times of the year when Mrs. McReady would have been most busy in her work, especially during the Christmas pantomime season.

Although Jane does not believe Sarah is a malevolent ghost, most people are frightened when they first come across her... they report inexplicable cold atmospheres and occasionally there will be a waft of very old-fashioned musky perfume, which is clearly defined, in a very limited space. Sometimes people standing in the wings will claim that someone has brushed past them, when there is no-one there. Quite often she will make herself felt at night, when there are deep shadows thrown by the winches, ropes and wooden panels behind the stage. One night a nightwatchman was terrified. He knew full well there was no-one else in the building, when a woman's voice shouted at him quite distinctly: 'Get out!' Needless to say, he did, and rapidly.

Other people have heard her whispering in their ear, not in an aggressive manner, but startling enough when you think you are alone...

Sometimes Sarah can be seen sitting in a particular box, perhaps the one which she used during her lifetime to watch performances. These sightings can be fleeting glimpses, so that when the person looks back a second later there is nothing to be seen. But Jane remembers one actor who was rehearsing on stage when he thought he saw Sarah. Later in the dressing room he was white with shock, because the apparition didn't go away.

At other times people just have a feeling about the box. Some time ago, Michael Bentine, who is President of ASSAP and well-known for his interest in psychic matters, visited the theatre to act in his own one man show. He knew nothing of the Old Vic's ghost, walked onto the stage

The Bristol Theatre Royal's Interior showing the haunted box..

and immediately pointed at that very box, saying that he felt very strongly that there was something there.

Jane's own interest in the ghost began when she spent a night alone in the theatre; until then she had not believed in ghosts, but she describes that occasion as 'a very haunted night', with several unexplained noises and lights swinging to and fro. She left at four in the morning, a quivering wreck. Some time later, she made the connection between the haunting and Sarah McReady, did a little research and discovered that her night alone had actually been the anniversary of Sarah's death. The next morning she stood on the stage and called into the empty theatre, 'Mrs McReady, it's you, isn't it?' Jane says she experienced an enormous wave of relief, as if Sarah was pleased that at last someone had acknowledged her.

It seems that Sarah McReady makes an unforgettable impression on everyone who experiences her performance, much as she did in life. Her reason for haunting seems to be her continuing interest in the fortunes of the Old Vic – and perhaps she simply wants to be remembered, and given the respect due to a redoubtable old lady who gave her life to the theatre. Of course, there is no absolute proof that the strange things happening in the Old Vic are due to a ghost and not to the active imaginations of actors in the throes of their imaginative craft... but Jane is convinced of Sarah's presence. She even lights candles for her in Bristol Cathedral, where Sarah McReady is buried with her husband, just to let her know she isn't forgotten... and perhaps to prevent her shouting at any more night-watchmen.

The Ancient Ram Inn

A whole book could be written about peculiar goings-on at the ancient Ram Inn at Wotten-Under-Edge. It is a building of great historical significance, and, like many old buildings, has acquired a long reputation for being horribly inhabited by a variety of mysterious presences – mostly malevolent.

John Humphries, the current owner, is a cheerful character who has great patience with the many paranormal investigators, foreign visitors, and the just-plain-curious who want to visit his haunted hostelry. Many researchers have made overnight stays at the Inn, and there have been a number of well-documented reports of strange happenings there.

The Ancient Ram Inn

The most dangerous room in which to spend a night is the bedchamber known as the Bishop's Room. Numerous reports tell of sudden, unexplained drops in temperature, often accompanied or followed by the presence of mysterious shapes – sometimes apparently male, sometimes very small and female – which appear when least expected. The experience frequently involves a sense of oppression, of something weighing down on the victim, or an apprehension of imminent disaster.

John has received many letters from guests who have slept – or, rather, not slept – in the Bishop's Room.

One guest wrote: 'At 5 a.m. I saw a white shape, approximately three feet in height. I was so shocked, I turned my head away. I then felt an icy breath on the left side of my face...'

For another guest the encounter was even more terrifying: 'At 12.20 a.m. I was aware that something strange was about to happen. I was drawn to look at the fireplace, where I saw a wispy white mist which developed into an outline of a woman. Later in the night, I felt a presence all around me. I tried to move my arms and open my eyes, but I couldn't. Something or someone was trying to pull me out of the bed...'

The experience is worst of all for the habitually courageous. 'At about 2.30 a.m.' wrote one victim, 'I woke up intending to have a glass of water from the sink. In the far corner I saw an appearance, or whatever, of a man in an old-fashioned night-gown, wearing an old and floppy cavalier hat. He was just standing there. I am not a man who is scared or spooked, so what I did was to walk towards him. I got to within about five feet of him – and then I got the shock of my life. He took a step towards me. I ducked between the two beds and sat down. I collected myself, told myself not to be so stupid, and stood up. At this point the man disappeared.' The writer finishes by saying, 'I was quite shaken by then, I had a glass of water, a cigarette and thought about it. I decided to say nothing about it, at the time.'

The Bishop's Room is not the only one which can fill overnight guests with abject terror. A gentleman staying in the Beaufort Room reported that he heard somebody walking up the stairs and along the landing towards the Berkeley Room, and one young man who slept in the Berkeley Room itself reported that in the early morning he awoke to feel a dog – well, some animal with four legs – standing on his chest. He moved, and he heard a thud as the animal jumped to the floor. But search the room as he might, he could find no trace of a living being...

And one guest who stayed in the Monk's Room asked desperately: 'Please let us know what was going on in the attic shortly after midnight. It sounded like someone was dragging furniture around for what seemed like an hour.'

John Humphries himself, during his twenty-six years living at the Ram Inn, has had many odd experiences, sometimes on his own, but often when he is with other people, who can corroborate his reports. Most of the happenings seem to have no cause or prompting, but one of John's accounts points to a possible cause of the unnatural phenomena.

About a year ago, one early evening, a young friend of John's had been apple-picking in John's garden and had come inside for a cup of tea. The lad commented on some stairs, which John had recently installed to give access to an old attic which he now used as his own bedroom. John had been told, many years before, by a medium, that a man called Tom had often slept in that attic room, and when he asked local villagers, they remembered Tom as a travelling horse-trader. On hearing the story, the lad commented that he had never had any contact with death until quite recently, when his uncle had died – and, he added, his uncle was known as Tom too...

At the mention of the name, there was a most alarming change in the atmosphere: a feeling of violent static charged the air. The radio, which had been playing quietly in the next room, suddenly blared out at maximum volume, and both John and his young friend felt such a weight hanging upon them that they thought their heads were going to split open. A few moments later, everything was quiet, but then the effects started again, dying away, only to recur a third time. John says that in all his time at the Inn, this is possibly the most frightening experience he has ever had, and he remains convinced that it was the mention of Tom the horse-trader's name that sparked the whole thing off.

With such a preponderance of apparently miscellaneous paranormal activity in one building, it comes as no surprise that someone seems to have captured a ghost on film. In July 1994, Ian Black and a team of fearless ghost hunters spent the night at the Ancient Ram and were surprised to discover, when their camera films were developed, that one print showed a ghostly image against a window. John Humphries explains that the image is that of an old woman who often appears at that window, someone whom mediums have described as a witch.

The notorious Bishop's Room at the Ram Inn

While the mysteries remain, there is, as it happens, one fail-safe method of observing phenomena in the Bishop's Room. It is one that requires considerable courage on behalf of the investigator who carries out the procedure.

First, all but one of the investigators must assemble in the dangerous Bishop's Room. The odd-person-out must then go down to the other end of the Inn, down a long and dark passageway, and all the lights in the whole building must be turned off. The lone investigator must then grope his way back to the others, remembering to tap along the floor with a stick, whilst avoiding bumping into all sorts of equipment and boxes left in the corridor. When this experiment was last attempted, researchers were eagerly waiting in the Bishop's Room with bated breath and in complete silence. Suddenly, an almighty crashing and banging interrupted the pervading quiet. Everybody jumped as the door to the room slowly swung open, but all heaved a sigh of relief when they realised that it wasn't a spook come to teach them a lesson, but the friendly face of their colleague, apologising for creating so much racket – he had fallen over a whole pile of equipment left standing in the corridor.

The Inn itself, and, perhaps, its ghosts, have every reason to be thankful for the existence and tolerance of John Humphries. The timber-framed Inn is believed to be nearly a thousand years old, and is in remarkably good condition for its age. The current owner, John (who is also in remarkably good condition for his age), took up residence in 1968, after Whitbread put the Inn up for sale. It is only by means of hard work and persistence that the Inn is still standing, for shortly after John moved in, he discovered that the local council wanted to knock down the building in order to widen the road. John fought a long campaign, and, aided by the local living residents, won the right to keep the Inn (and its mysterious inhabitants) from the bulldozer and from total destruction.

Warminster
– UFOs and Crop Circles –
or Something Else?

During the 1960s the location around Warminster became famous for UFO reports and sightings. There was so much publicity generated that a sort of psychic pilgrimage to the reported spots developed, where everybody hoped to see something out of the ordinary. In latter years, the focus of attention was on crop circles, which of course were far less elusive, and visually very exciting. The publicity was even more intense and instead of there being a pilgrimage, the visits to the crop circles were more of a mass rally – people from all walks of life, and from many other countries came to visit this phenomenon.

Of course, the case for the crop circles all but collapsed with the confessions of various hoaxers – they had fooled many, including some hardened sceptics. However it is understandable how belief in such stories can suddenly proliferate: during the hectic 'UFO flap' in Warminster at the time, just about any apparently unusual occurrence was immediately attributed to alien intervention, often without any real investigation into alternative explanations. It is also possible that witnesses unwittingly tailored their reports to fit other UFO stories that they had heard.

UFO stories still occasionally occur, and often fit into the classic pattern for such stories. The case of Mr and Mrs Poole combines many such classic elements, with one or two chilling extra details...

For many months during 1965, a number of witnesses around different parts of the Warminster area complained of some very alarming loud noises which seemed to have no apparent natural or human explanation. The noises sometimes had a droning or throbbing element. Some of the witnesses also spoke of seeing very bright flashes of light, some of which were described as large orange balls of fire.

In the November of 1965, Mr and Mrs Poole were driving into Warminster late at night to pick up their daughter from a party. As they passed beneath one of the bridges into the city, Mr Poole had to take evasive action to avoid what looked like a drunken man, sprawled in the middle of the road. Concerned that the man might be injured by other less alert drivers, he stopped the car and got out to see of he could move the drunk onto the pavement. When he walked back to the spot where he thought the man had been, there was nobody there. The Pooles were puzzled, and not a little upset, for they had both been utterly convinced that they had seen someone in the middle of the road.

They continued their journey and collected their daughter without further incident, and all three then drove back along the same route. Close to the same spot on the road where they thought they had seen the drunk, Mr Poole couldn't help noticing a large ball of orange light, quite stationary, resting on the bridge embankment. At the same time, Mr Poole's engine began to misfire, and despite having his foot on the accelerator, the car slowed down to a jerking, coughing, crawl.

The orange ball, which had been stationary, now seemed to slide down the embankment and stopped in front of the car, which was still jerking along. Mr Poole had the impression that it was rotating at great speed in front of him. Suddenly the ball shot off at a tangent upwards, and as it did so, the car roared into life.

A sketch of the UFO that was encountered by Mr and Mrs Poole

Despite these extraordinary occurrences, Mr Poole noticed some other odd things happening. Firstly, there was another object on the bridge; spherical like the other, but much darker, but he was dazzled by the light from the orange ball and was unable to make out much detail. The car was now behaving normally, and he drove away from the spot at high speed, concerned to put as much distance between himself and that mysterious location as possible.

Mr Poole's story is quite disturbing, but it is absolutely typical of many reports around the Warminster area during the mid 1960s. Without doubt, the 'orange ball' seen by Mr Poole was a UFO in the truest sense. It must be remembered that UFO actually stands for 'Unidentified Flying Object'; not 'Alien Spaceship'. The orange ball could just as easily have been a natural – though rare – occurrence, such as a ball of lightning, or a ball of gas: either event could conceivably have affected the operation of Mr Poole's car, by interfering with the ignition system, or adversely affecting the gas mixture in the carburettor.

As for the man, sprawling in the road; this event, taken on its own, sounds very typical of the 'Phantom Hitch-hiker' phenomenon such as that which happened at Bluebell Hill (see introduction). This may have actually been a genuine paranormal event, but one which became wrapped up with other happenings. There are many documented cases where the driver and/or passengers are utterly convinced that they have seen, or even worse, hit a pedestrian. But when they get out of the car – there is nobody to be found...

Recommended Further Reading

Allen, Thomas

> Possessed
> Doubleday 1993

Evans, Hilary

> Gods, Spirits, Cosmic Guardians
> Aquarian Press 1987

Gould, Alan and Cornell,A.D.

> Poltergeists
> Routldge and Kegan Paul 1979

Goss, Michael

> The Evidence for Phantom Hitchhikers
> ASSAP 1992

Hole, Christina

> Haunted England
> Fitzhouse Books 1940

Moberley, C.A.E.
and Jourdain, E.F

> The Ghosts of the Trianon
> Aquarian Press 1988

Perry, Michael (ed.)

> Deliverance
> SPCK 1987

Playfair, Guy Lyon

> The Flying Cow
> Souvenir Press 1975

Playfair, Guy Lyon

> The Infinite Boundary
> Souvenir Press 1977

Poole, Keith

> Britain's Haunted Heritage
> Robert Hale 1988

Seymour, Deryck

> The Ghosts of Berry Pomeroy Castle
> Obelisk Publications 1994

Spencer,
John and Anne

> Encyclopedia of Ghosts and Spirits
> Headline 1992

Spencer, John and Wells, Tony — Ghost Watching
Virgin 1994

Whitaker, Terence — England's Ghostly Heritage
Robert Hale 1989

Wilson, Colin — Poltergeist
New England Library 1981